MW01048074

"BE EXTRAORDINARY!"

The Teenager's Roadmap to Success!

_____

DARRYL ROSS

_____

Positive Praise!

"Darryl Ross is amazing! He truly impacts America's Youth!"
—Kristi Frank, NBC's *The Apprentice*, Season One

"Darryl Ross is one of the best speakers I've ever heard. He truly made a difference in the students' lives."
—Patty Reid, Teacher, Young Scholar's Academy, Fort Mohave, AZ

"Darryl is very knowledgeable and made our event educational. I would highly recommend Darryl Ross for any student function!"
—Debbie Hiestand, PTA Chairman, Fort Mohave, AZ

"Darryl Ross was very motivating and knowledgeable. My students really seemed to enjoy his presentation and hope he comes back soon. I recommend Mr. Darryl Ross for any high school or college event."
—Mehdi Afiat, Ph.D., Professor of Economics, College of Southern Nevada

"Thank you for helping us in our career hunt. I had given up, but your expertise and motivating words will help me get back out there and get the job I want."
—Dane Beebe, Student, College of Southern Nevada

"Darryl Ross has an insight into the human condition that allows you to grow to the next level in your life. His clear and concise motivational steps will take you from your current life situation to an extraordinary life."
—Mike Gallo, President, Red Rock Ltd.

Be Extraordinary

Copyright © 2012

All rights reserved. No part of this book may be reproduced or transmitted in any form without expressed written permission of the author, except for brief quotations used in reviews written specifically for inclusion in a newspaper, magazine, or on the Internet.

Printed in the United States of America

Edited by: Joana Asala / Compassrose.com

Cover by: Christopher Adams / Kgraphik.com

Supported by: Career Transition For Dancers
Hubbard Street Dance 1147 W. Jackson Blvd
Chicago, IL 60607
www.careertransition.org

About the Author

Darryl Ross is a graduate from James Madison University and began his career in the entertainment industry. As a lead singer and emcee, Ross was hired by the Department of Defense to perform in U.S.O. shows for the military. Ross and his troop King's Six performed in South Korea, Okinawa, and Japan.

From there, Ross performed for Royal Caribbean and Cunard cruise lines. Finally, he worked in the casino circuit as a featured performer in Lake Tahoe, Atlantic City, and Las Vegas. In addition, Darryl was featured on the E! Entertainment network and the Travel Channel.

After leaving the stage, Darryl worked as the entertainment reporter for Fox 5 News in Las Vegas. He covered the red carpet for the Billboard Music Awards, Country Music Awards, and the MTV Video Music Awards. He interviewed such stars as Celine Dion, Seal, Tim McGraw, Faith Hill, and music mogul Clive Davis.

Today, Darryl travels the country, speaking at middle schools, high schools, and youth organizations. He's given hundreds of motivational presentations for groups of ten people to one thousand! He is the author of the motivational audio CD *Be Extraordinary* and a contributing author to the book *Jumpstart Your Success.*

"BE EXTRAORDINARY!"

The Teenager's Roadmap to Success!

DARRYL ROSS

Table of Contents

To my loving wife Jennifer.
Thank you for your love and support!

Dedicated to my children:

Javon Daylen Ross and Jazmine Faith Ross

Message to Parents and Educators

I truly enjoy speaking with teenagers. For some reason, I connect with teens—probably because I'm a big kid myself. I understand that most teenagers have two distinct versions of themselves. The first version can be challenging. This teenager thinks he or she knows it all and will say or do anything to be cool. That's right! This teenage version is only interested in *not showing* his or her vulnerability. This can be frustrating to an adult!

But understand this: The other version of that exact same teenager needs you! He or she has goals, dreams, and, most importantly, is scared to death! It's our job as adults to *connect with them* and *not* make them connect with us!

How Do You Do That?

1. Show up!

It's difficult to connect with anyone if you're never around. Adults are very busy and can't be everywhere. But schedule the time. Because of work, there were times I had to miss my son's soccer practice or game. (He understood.) But when I scheduled a future game and put it on my calendar, I would not break it! I was there!

2. Create an atmosphere of unconditional love!

Most teens believe they are only loved *if* they get good grades, *if* they do their chores, *if* they make the team. Obviously, getting good grades and doing chores is part of teenage life. But don't judge their *overall worth* if they forget to take out the trash. Teenagers want unconditional love!

3. Speak to teens with respect!

I know it can be challenging, but teenagers are people.
And no one (teenager or adult) likes to be *barked at* and
spoken to as if they are complete idiots! After a long day
at work, most adults come home and have little patience.
(I understand this because I have two kids.) But try to
slow down and watch your tone!

4. Teen concerns are important!

Teen concerns may seem silly to us, but they really matter
to them! Let them express their feelings! Adults verbally
say, "We care about teen issues," but we *show* teens that
we *don't* care by interrupting, not letting them talk,
rolling our eyes, or multitasking while they're talking.
When adults do this, teens feel as if they're not being
heard and will slowly start to withdraw. Months later,
you'll wonder why your son or daughter never opens up
to you!

You'd be surprised how these simple actions make a
world of difference to a teenager. Please understand: I am
not implying that we shouldn't have discipline at home or
school. Teenagers will run all over you if they don't sense
structure and boundaries. I'm simply stating that adults
need to step up and make more of an effort to connect
with teenagers. I know you may not like their music, but
make an effort to listen to a few tunes. You would be
surprised how teens react when they think you know or
have at least listened to their music. Ask their opinion on
certain topics and engage with them in activities.

Don't forget—you were once a teenager, too! Do you remember how you felt about adults? Today's teen feels the exact same way!

I had a presentation set for a non-profit organization in Arlington, Virginia. The non-profit's sole purpose was to assist disabled young adults and help find them jobs. The VP of the organization saw me at a different event and hired me to give my "Be Extraordinary" motivational talk to the disabled group.

I arrived the morning of the presentation, but the VP was not there yet. However, the onsite supervisor met me. He pulled me into a conference room with two of his assistants and went on a rant about how he didn't think this presentation was appropriate. Raising his voice, he told me he felt as if they were too mentally challenged and that this would be *over their heads!* He was completely opposed to me giving my presentation. I tried to explain that the VP invited me and specifically wanted that presentation. He didn't care. He said *he* was the supervisor! I did my best to calm him down. I explained that I'm very experienced and would do my best to keep the material fun, easy, and relevant. Finally, he agreed to let me give my talk.

In my mind, I was thinking, "What have I gotten myself into? I can't change my material now!" The VP told me the audience would be comprised of disabled people. The supervisor acted as if they were so mentally challenged that they wouldn't understand what I was saying! What was I going to do? If they couldn't understand me, what was I doing there? I was truly worried about it being a disaster, but it was too late to back out. The audience was waiting! About that time, the VP walked in and introduced me. Because he had just arrived, I did not have the opportunity to ask him about what the supervisor had said.

Oh, well! With the VP in the back of the room and the supervisor still glaring at me, I started my presentation for about one hundred people. Guess what? It went great! They were awesome! They asked questions, we laughed, cried, and had a great time. Yes, the group had disabilities. Some people were in wheelchairs, others had amputated arms, and others were mentally challenged, but they all still had goals and they all still had dreams!

Afterwards, the VP asked the group if they would like me to come back next year, and they all cheered "yes!" As the audience was leaving, almost everyone came up to get a copy of my book and shake my hand. Surprisingly, even the supervisor shook my hand. Can you believe that? Finally, I got the chance to *gently* explain to the VP what happened earlier with the supervisor. The VP was not surprised and said, *"It's a shame that we have supervisors and educators that place their own limitations on what's possible in other people."* He then asked if I was available to give the same presentation for their sister property in Washington, DC. I was thrilled!

I think this is a great reminder to challenge the teenagers in your life. Don't label them by placing your own limiting belief on their true ability. Whether they are disabled or not, they can achieve more—they want to achieve more!

Message to Teenagers

"Because the street's a short stop. Either you're slingin' crack rock or you got a wicked jumpshot."
—Notorious B.I.G.

Don't believe the hype! There is much more to teenage life than "dealin', ballin', or shot callin'!"

Question: Do you want to be unique and stand out from the crowd?

Answer: Then don't follow the crowd!

Don't get me wrong. If you have strong relationships with good, supportive friends, that's awesome! Keep it going!

If not, understand this: It's easier to follow the crowd and do drugs. It's easier to follow the crowd and drink alcohol. It's easier to *not* study or practice and follow the crowd. It takes courage to do the right thing, stand up for yourself, and *not* follow the crowd.

Whether you realize it or not, if you associate with people who have no dreams, who have no goals for their lives, and who continue to make poor decisions...*so will you!*

According to Author Jim Rohn, *"Your overall success will be an average of the five people you spend the most time with."*

Makes you think twice about who you hang with, doesn't it? Take a second to think about your five closest friends. What are *their* goals? What are *their* dreams? Do they know *your* dreams? As they say, "You are who you roll with." Choose to "roll with" good friends.

Another way to be unique and stand out from the crowd is to take pride in everything you do! I'm going to say that again: Take pride in everything you do! Not just the things you like to do or mandatory things from school— *everything!*

I know this might be difficult, but *attack* your homework, after school practice, and your household chores, such as raking leaves, mowing lawns, cleaning your room, etc. This shows maturity and that you're responsible! It doesn't mean you like it, it simply means you're mature. It means you're *extraordinary!*

The crowd will tell you:
- "Your household chores don't matter."
- "Forget your homework!"
- "Who cares about cleaning your room or practicing?"

As you continue on your life journey, you'll notice successful young men and women have the ability to focus, work hard, and take pride in everything they do.

Because they *don't* follow the crowd, they will:
- Go to college.
- Serve our country in the military.
- Become doctors or nurses.
- Become premiere athletes or musicians.
- Start their own companies.
- Work in fulfilling careers.

So can you!

In ancient times, farmers would dig ditches in their land to prepare for the rainy season. This would be an area in the land to capture the rain so the farmer had water for his family, crops, and livestock.

It was challenging because the farmer had to dig the ditches in the middle of the summer, months before the rainy season. Even though it was blistering hot outside, the farmer worked in advance and prepared the land so he was ready when the rain came. This is a great reminder of the principle of preparation!

Reading through this book works in the exact same way! You're preparing (in advance) for great things to come. Read each chapter and reflect on what you learn. Be sure to fill out the questions at the end of each chapter.
You may not receive any immediate gratification, but stick with it. Just like the farmer, you're getting ready for the rain to come! It's time to "dig your ditches!"

Let's Get Started!

> "All our dreams can come true if we have the courage to pursue them."
>
> **Walt Disney**

From "A" to Dreams!

It's all about dreams. Nothing great has ever been accomplished without it first starting as a dream. When you were a kid, what did you want to be when you grew up? Maybe you wanted to be a firefighter, veterinarian, football player, or a prima ballerina. The best part about dreams is that you can be whatever you want to be. And most kids truly believe their dreams will come true. But as you get a little older, your dreams start to vanish. Ask yourself this question: What happened to my dreams?

Many teenagers have stopped dreaming about their future. Why? Because they feel as if they don't have enough money, that they're not smart enough, pretty enough, or even good enough. Life starts to wear them down, and all their dreams wear down, too.

Don't let this happen to you! Dreams are the most magical power that you have. Your mind is the one place you can go where *anything* is possible.

As a kid, I was the ultimate daydreamer. I pictured myself scoring touchdowns in the NFL, being a zoologist, and definitely singing in a sold-out concert arena. I liked sports, animals, and I loved to sing! But professional singing was not at the top of my dad's career list for his children. I grew up in a military family with my older brother and younger sister, so discipline and hard work were the songs we sang. Actually, my mom and dad liked music, but they liked straight A's in school even more. It was tough "fitting in" at school because we moved every two years to a new city and new military base. It seemed like I was always the "new kid" on the block. Believe it or not, I was born in Okinawa, Japan. I always

felt like a true outsider!
Have you ever gone to a brand-new school where you didn't know anyone? I remember moving to Virginia from North Carolina just before my sophomore year in high school. I was scared to death!

On the first day of school, my brother, sister, and I walked down the street from our house to wait for the school bus. We didn't know exactly where the bus stop was; we just knew it was at the end of the street. I was so nervous. And to make it worse, it was pouring rain and we had no umbrella. I noticed all the other kids were waiting for the bus across the street under a dry carport. It was a guy named Bobby's house, and he had no intention of inviting the new kids to come over and get out of the rain. I'll never forget those ten or twelve kids snickering, pointing, and whispering as we stood outside getting totally drenched. I was hoping some of the kids would call us over, introduce themselves, and welcome us to the neighborhood. Somebody, please. Somebody? Anybody? No one did! Eventually, the bus came and took us to school. It seemed like the worst day of my life. I had no umbrella, and I definitely didn't have any friends, but I still had my dreams.

So do you! No matter what you're going through, your dreams belong to you! I dreamed that I knew more people at school, dreamed that I was popular, and I dreamed that I would win the school talent show for singing.
That's right! The high school talent contest was the following month, and since I didn't know anyone, I figured I should enter the contest. Guess what? I won! It was great! Part of me was shocked, but the other part remembered that I dreamed I would win! After winning the contest, I slowly started to make friends. Funny thing,

even those kids at the bus stop changed their tune and wanted to be friends. Imagine that!

By my senior year, my musical ability led me to James Madison University in Harrisonburg, Virginia. And yes, I sang in every singing group on campus. I sang in the university chorus, gospel choir, and I even started my own R&B band. Four years later, I received my bachelor's in communications, but my dream was to keep singing—so I did! I feel blessed to have performed professionally for twenty years. I performed onboard luxury ships for Royal Caribbean and Cunard cruise lines, in musical theater productions, and even huge casinos in Atlantic City, Reno, Lake Tahoe, and Las Vegas.

But by far, my favorite experience was the U.S.O. shows for the military. My band performed on different military bases for the troops in the South Pacific. Have you ever heard of Mount Suribachi? If not, just think of that famous pose with a few marines pushing up the American flag. That's in Iwo Jima! And that mountain is called Mount Suribachi. We performed on top of that mountain for 2000 marines—it was truly an amazing experience! After growing up as a military kid, who would have thought that I would sing on military bases around the world as an adult? *That's* the power of dreams!

The great thing about dreams...you can have as many dreams as you want! For me, after retiring from the stage, it was my dream to work as an entertainment reporter. After so many years on stage, it seemed like a perfect fit to interview people and develop news stories around entertainers. I was lucky enough to get a job at KVVU Fox 5 News in Las Vegas. Over the years, I interviewed some of the biggest names in entertainment. My favorites were Celine Dion, Kanye West, Seal, Carrie Underwood,

Kelly Clarkson, Jason Mraz, Taylor Swift, David Copperfield, Tim McGraw, and Faith Hill.

But before I worked for Fox 5 News, my dream was to start my own entertainment television show. I wanted to host the show and interview the hottest musical acts that came to Las Vegas. It would be like the Access Hollywood for the music business. The original title of the show was called *Soundcheck*.

Las Vegas is a great place to see concerts! On any given weekend, we could have four or five major recording artists performing in different venues on the same night. My vision was to bring cameras to the arena and capture a quick interview before or after the act's sound check. We would keep the show all about music, their tour, and songwriting—absolutely no tabloid talk! I wanted cool music and really tight editing. I wrote out my entire idea on a piece of paper. And then I thought, "Now what?"

How can I possibly get my dream TV show on the air? Who had the money? Who had a camera? I had no idea how to do this, but I believed 100% that my dream could be done. I shared my idea with everyone and slowly started to meet people in the television industry. Before I knew it, I partnered with a television producer and a very talented cameraman. We all had the same vision for the show and agreed to develop it together. We decided to call the show *On Tour*. We designed a great logo, filmed the basic intro, and actually wrote our own theme song for the show. And then I thought, "Now what?"

We needed a superstar interview for our video demo reel. But how could we get such an interview? We had no contacts or powerful friends in the music business.

Driving home one day, I heard on the radio that the World Music Awards would be in Las Vegas over the summer. That was it! I knew if we could somehow get into the award show, we could land plenty of great interviews. But how? Once again, I had no idea, but I believed 100% that my dream could be done. We called the phone number on the World Music Awards website. We were told that only established television shows would be given press passes for admission to the red carpet. We called the next day, and the next, and the next. We were told to forget it!

About two days before the award show, we called again and were accidentally transferred to the executive producer's direct line. I love accidents that help you! After a brief conversation, the executive producer agreed to give total unknowns press passes to the World Music Awards. I was so excited! Two days later, I was standing on the red carpet next to the hosts of TV shows such as *E.T.* and *Access Hollywood.* And, more importantly, I interviewed superstars like Toby Keith Chris Brown, Sugar Ray, Josh Groban, Usher, and Clive Davis. My TV show *On Tour* was born.

Over the next few years, I interviewed some of the hottest pop, rock, country, and hip hop acts in the world. I also covered the red carpet at the Billboard Music Awards, Country Music Awards, and the MTV Video Music Awards. Our show aired in Las Vegas on KVVU Fox 5 every Friday night. It helped me land a job as their entertainment reporter.

Lesson learned:

Dream big!

Write down five of your dreams.

Don't be afraid to dream big! There is no such thing as too big of a dream! Go for it!

1.)_____

2.)_____

3.)_____

4.)_____

5.)_____

"The greatest discovery of my generation is that human beings can alter their lives by altering their attitudes."

William James

Attitude = Achievement

Attitude is everything! You don't get what you deserve, you get what you expect! What do you expect for yourself? Your attitude is one of the strongest attributes you can develop. You can't control what other people think or what they say, but you can control how *you* feel—it's *your* attitude!

"Attitude shapes your behavior."

Have you noticed that very successful people have extraordinary attitudes? They are not better than you or smarter than you. But for some reason, they seem to have a positive attitude, even if things aren't going well. Why? Because they understand the success principle. It's called the 20 / 80 principle!

Here is the 20 / 80 principle:

Only 20% of your success or achievement comes from actual skill or ability. Did you know that? You could be an athlete, doctor, lawyer, teacher, or a high school student. It doesn't matter! If you're really good at science, math, or soccer, only 20% of your success in those areas is actual skill.

Eighty percent is your attitude! That's right! The real power is your *attitude* towards science, math, or soccer. Wouldn't it be great if you had a dream or goal for your life and your first reaction was "yes" you could achieve it? Literally, from day one, you truly believed you could accomplish your goal. Unfortunately, most teenagers do not think this way. Most teens (and many adults, too) think of an idea or goal for their life and within minutes they start thinking of all the reasons they can't do it.

Can I get an A in this class? No!
Can I graduate? No!
Can I get into college? Absolutely not!

I'm proud to tell you that the true answer is yes, you can! How would it feel to know that your biggest obstacles for your life are your own limiting beliefs?

Can I get an A in this class? **Yes!**
Can I graduate? **Yes!**
Can I get into college? **Absolutely, yes!**

But it will take some training, and, most importantly, it will take re-conditioning of your mind because your external world has all the power—so far!

"No one talks to you more than you."

Here are three key steps to shape your attitude:

1.) Believe in yourself! You have greatness within you! You have yet to realize your full potential. You have incredible gifts, talents, and abilities! Believe it!

2.) Beware of vampires! That's right—vampires! There are certain people in your life who are toxic, who will suck the dreams right out of you. Don't let your fellow student, friend, or even a loved one poison your dream.

Ralph Waldo Emerson said, *"Why should my happiness depend on the thoughts of what's going on in someone else's head?"*

3.) Positive in = Positive out! Your attitude relects the way you think about yourself. You may not be perfect, but if you think of yourself in a positive way, you will have a positive light. But the opposite is also true. If you think of yourself in a negative way, you will have a negative light.

Negative in = Negative out! Keep a positive mindset!

Let's be honest. Sometimes you have a negative light because you're afraid. I know you don't want to admit it, but it's natural to be afraid. Maybe you're afraid or nervous about an upcoming test, baseball tryout, or job interview. Fear is completely natural. But work through it! Don't let your fear dictate your actions!

What is fear?

F – False
E – Evidence
A – Appearing
R – Real

FEAR will convince you that your dream is not possible. Have you ever had a dream or goal for your life and *you* let *you* talk *yourself* out of it? That happens to all of us! But here's the good news! If you can talk yourself out of it, you can talk yourself *into* it. It's all in the power of your mind!

Have you ever heard of Roger Bannister? He was the first human to run the mile under four minutes. Keep in mind, this was not a mere sports record, this was something that had never been done before.
Kinesiologists, sports doctors, and other premier athletes

all agreed that it was humanly impossible to run the mile in under four minutes. Roger was told that his heart and lungs would explode!

Guess what? On May 6th, 1954, Roger Bannister broke the four-minute barrier by running the mile in 3:59. That's not the amazing part. The amazing part is that within one year, several others ran the mile in under four minutes, too. To this day, over 100,000 people have broken that record, including some high school and middle school teenagers.

What happened? Did everyone just start to run faster one day? How can a record that stood for thousands of years now be broken all the time?

Answer: Their inner beliefs changed. Their attitude changed from it being impossible to possible.

Thomas Carlisle said, *"Be careful what you think about because you will surely get it."*

Lesson learned:

Shift your attitude!

Write down five areas where you need to work on your attitude.

Here are some examples: dealing with a fellow student, one of your difficult classes, a sport, a musical instrument.

1.)_____

2.)_____

3.)_____

4.)_____

5.)_____

> **"If you don't know where you're going, how can you expect to get there?"**
>
> **Basil S. Walsh**

Reach Beyond Your Reach!

As a teenager, if you want to reach your full potential, you *must* challenge yourself. That means stretch an extra inch, run an extra mile, or study an extra hour. If your goal is ten reps, change it to fifteen.

To "reach beyond your reach" means you should set your goals high! Famous author and speaker Les Brown said:

"People don't fail because they set their goals too high and miss...they fail because they set their goals too low and hit."

I don't believe teenagers set their goals low on purpose. Most teens don't even realize they are setting their goals low. I believe they set their goals low because they are trying to be reasonable. They will consider the achievements and goals of other teens in their circle and make their goals similar.

I remember taking a higher-level math class my sophomore year in college. The consensus on campus was no one ever gets an "A" in Dr. Woal's class. Because of this, I just assumed the typical "A" student would get a "B," and "B" students (like me) would get a "C." What grade do you think I got? You guessed it: a "C."
I later found out that the rumor on campus was completely wrong. Plenty of students got A's. But I talked myself into a "C" because I was being reasonable with my goals. *Never* let anyone else determine your goal!

Question: What's the first step in accomplishing your goals?

Answer: Write down your goals.

There is power behind putting your goals on paper. According to the book *Look Within or Do Without* by Tom Bay, the Harvard Business School did a study on the financial status of its students 10 years after graduation.

Here's the breakdown of the study:

27% of the Harvard graduates needed financial assistance.

60% of the Harvard graduates were living paycheck to paycheck.

10% of the Harvard graduates were living comfortably.

Only 3% of the Harvard graduates were financially independent.

The study also looked at goal setting and found lightning in a bottle!

The 27% that needed financial assistance had absolutely no goal-setting process in their lives.

The 60% living paycheck to paycheck had minimal goals such as, *"How can I get my next paycheck?"*

The 10% that were living comfortably had more general goals. They knew where they wanted to be in five years.

But the 3% that were financially independent had written down their goals and the steps required to reach them.

Here's a bonus: The 3% that were financially independent had more financial wealth than the other 97% *combined!*

Effective goal setting starts with the S.M.A.R.T Goal System.

S – Specific
M – Measurable
A – Achievable
R – Relevant
T – Timed

Specific

Be specific! It could be to get an "A" in trigonometry, make the basketball team, or lose ten pounds.
This may sound crazy, but you would be surprised how many teenagers attempt great things in their lives but never clearly state their goal. They'll just wander around in "vague-ville."

Clearly defining your goal gives you vision. During World War II, military commanders would speak of an objective or their goal in a particular battle. Former NFL coach Tony Dungy often spoke of their clear team goals and their specific game plan. Some of your favorite authors will use the title to their book as their goal. Authors will often write the title to their book first, even if it's just a working title. So while they're writing their book, if they ever get off course, they can simply re-read their title to give them direction.

It's imperative that you clearly state your objective. Clearly define your goal!

Measurable

Your goal must be measurable. If there is no way to measure your goal, how will you know when you have achieved it?

For example:

Your goal can't be "I need to lose weight and get in shape." That's not measurable! It should be "I'm going to lose ten pounds by summer" or "I'm going to run the mile in six minutes!"

Your goal can't be "I need to make more money." It should be "I'm going to make $300 a week working part time" or "I'm going to make an extra $1000 a month."

You decide the amount, but make it specific and measureable!

Achievable

Your goal should be high and challenging but attainable. This does not mean you should lower your standards or make your goal easy to achieve. It simply means you should be realistic.

I don't think a goal of being a doctor without college or medical training is realistic. But if your goal is to study hard, get good grades, go to college and then medical school, then being a heart surgeon is very achievable!

Relevant

Why is your goal relevant to you? Why do you want it? You can break through barriers and overcome any obstacle if you have enough reasons!

Show me someone with a strong, relevant reason, and I'll show you someone who *will* achieve their goal. Why is your goal so important to you?

> *"There are no right or wrong why's — just strong or weak why's!"*
> **—Professor Joe Martin**

Whatever it is, make your "why" or your reason for achieving your goal compelling! No one is ever truly successful because they are somewhat interested in their goal. Not a chance! They are successful because they know their "why" and it is an absolute must. Why do you want it? *Why?*

Timed

Write down the date you *will* achieve your goal and sign it! When are you going to do it? Six weeks? Six months? Two years? It doesn't matter when, just decide and sign it! You have now created a contract with yourself. Whenever you look at your goal sheet, you'll see the goal, achievement date, and your signature.

Don't forget to write down your action steps!

Let's say your specific goal is to make the high school basketball team as a shooting guard and average ten points a game. Great!

Your action steps could be to practice an extra hour a day, attend a basketball training camp, or ask your basketball coach for tips on fundamentals. There are many different action steps you can take, but the bottom line is you have to do it!

Lesson learned:

Set your goals high!

"The reason most people never reach their goals is that they don't define them or ever seriously consider them as believable or achievable. Winners can tell you where they are going, what they plan to do along the way, and who will be sharing the adventure with them."

Denis Watley

(Think about your goals and write them down!)

Write down your specific and measurable one-year goals.

1.)_____

2.)_____

3.)_____

Write down three action steps for your one-year goals.

1.)_____

2.)_____

3.)_____

Why do you want to achieve your one-year goals?

_____

_____

_____

DATE YOU WILL ACHIEVE THESE GOALS:

_____

SIGN NAME: _____

Write down your specific and measurable five-year goals.

1.)_____

2.)_____

3.)_____

Write down three action steps for your five-year goals.

1.)_____

2.)_____

3.)_____

Why do you want to achieve your five-year goals?

_____

_____

_____

_____

DATE YOU WILL ACHIEVE THESE GOALS

_____

SIGN NAME: _____

**Congratulations!
You just signed a contract with
yourself!**

"It's not how much smarts you have, it's how much HEART you have!"

James Malinchak

It's Not About Your Age, It's About Your Desire!

It's truly amazing how far you can get with just one thing: Desire! Think about the goals you wrote down in the last chapter: How bad do you want it? Are you willing to work for it? Are you willing to sweat for it?

Take a mental picture of your goal. Now ask yourself these questions:
- What am I waiting on?
- Why haven't I started on my goal?

Your goal could be to get straight A's on your next report card, make the cheerleading team, or get accepted into college. Whatever your goal, there is always something you can do *today* to help you achieve it. Sometimes teenagers believe they are too young to start working on their dreams. But in reality, there is no reason you can't start planting the seeds for success today!

It's not about your age, it's about your desire!

Have you ever considered working as a news reporter? What are you waiting on? You could start your own newspaper in your hometown. Don't wait to use a computer, write it out by hand. Then go door to door in your neighborhood and sell the newspaper for fifty cents an issue. Does that sound crazy?

Brennan LaBrie, born in 1999, started his own newspaper in Port Townsend, Washington. He writes *The Spruce Street Weekly* by hand and sells it every Saturday in his neighborhood. Currently, he has over 200 customers! *Time for Kids* magazine heard about Brennan and invited him to cover the 2010 Winter Olympics in Vancouver. He was the youngest journalist at the Olympics. Brennan

Labrie was just twelve years old.

It's not about your age, it's about your desire!

Do you love animals? Have you ever considered working in a zoo or veterinarian office? What are you waiting on? You could research the anatomy of animals at the library or on the Internet. Volunteer at your local veterinarian's office and, hopefully, assist the veterinarian doctor. Does that sound crazy?

Courtney Oliver from Olympia, Washington, would go to the library with her mom to research the anatomy of dogs and cats. Every Saturday, she would volunteer at her local veterinarian's office. Her job was to sweep the hallways, take out the trash, and clean all the cages. Over time, the doctors trusted Courtney to walk the animals to the evaluation rooms. Eventually, she sat in on major surgeries. In 2010, Courtney completed an online course, giving her a certification as a veterinarian assistant. Courtney Oliver was just eleven years old.

It's not about your age, it's about your desire!

Have you ever considered being a pilot? What are you waiting on? After school, you could work for extra money, pay for flight lessons, and hopefully, become a pilot. Does that sound crazy?

Jonathan Strickland is from Compton, California, and dreamed of being a pilot. For months after school, Jonathan earned money washing cars and mowing lawns in his neighborhood. He took his money to a flight training school in San Diego. The instructors were so impressed they gave Jonathan a full scholarship to the school, where he earned his pilot's license.

As of today, Jonathan is in the *Guinness Book of World Records* for being the youngest person to ever pilot a single-engine plane and a helicopter on the same day. Jonathan Strickland was just fourteen years old.

Jonathan Strickland - Timeline

2006- 14 years old:

1st aircraft solo (Cessna 152) – record holder, youngest to achieve
1st helicopter solo (Robinson R22) – record holder youngest to achieve)
1st International helicopter trip from Los Angeles to Vancouver, Canada – record holder
1st same day aircraft & helicopter solo – record holder, youngest to achieve

2007 – 15 years old:

Introduced & learned to flying a high performance complex aircraft
Learned how to fly using Garmin's G1000

2008 – 16 years old:

Earned Student Pilot Certificate
Flown over 100hrs form Solo at the age of 16, to Private on 17th birthday

2009 – 17 years old: Flew a Cessna from Los Angeles Ca, to Atlanta Ga. (16hr trip

Lesson learned:

It's about your desire!

Write down your top three career choices.

What career would you love to have? What do you want to be?

1.)_____

2.)_____

3.)_____

Write down the top three reasons you *have not* started.

1.)_____

2.)_____

3.)_____

Write down three things you could do today, then start!

1.)_____

2.)_____

3.)_____

> **"Focus on your hits, not your strikeouts!"**
>
> **Darryl Ross**

Focus, Focus, Focus!

Don't let yourself become distracted. It can be difficult to focus as a teenager because you are surrounded by the most exciting, tempting, stressful, awesome people and gadgets anywhere in the world. Think about your cell phone for a minute. Just a few years ago, your cell could do two things: make and receive phone calls. Now, you can play games, music, text, e-mail, take pictures, shoot video, and go on the Internet. Just owning a cell phone is very distracting!

Focus is the key! You must learn to mentally "stay in the moment!" If you're at football practice, focus on football. If you're in art class, focus on art. And if you're in biology, focus on biology.

Some teenagers may say, "I've got too much going on; I can't control my mind." **Yes, you can!** You are much more resilient than you think. But you have to work at it and condition yourself. Ask yourself these questions:

- How do I react in a crisis or a stressful situation?
- What's the first emotion?
- Do I get angry?
- Do I yell and scream?
- Do I cry? Get emotional?
- Do I internalize everything and barely react?

Once you have figured out your trait, understand this: In times of crisis, you will go to that trait *every single time!* It doesn't make it right; it's just what you are accustomed to doing. I hear many people say, "That's just how I am." Not true—it's a choice!

Whether you realize it or not, you *choose* your actions based on how you physically and emotionally feel. If you're happy, sad, tired, hungry, or pressured, it will affect your overall attitude. But you also *choose* your actions based on what you are mentally focusing on. You can *choose* to focus on "I can't do it." Or you can *choose* to focus on "I can do it." It's an absolute choice!

According to philosophy expert Dr. Nathaniel Branden, we should all live more consciously! Dr. Branden has a PhD in Psychology and is a pioneer in the field of self-esteem and personal development. He says, "It's a proven psychological fact that just being observant of how you're performing in a certain area of your life…will actually improve that area." Start to observe yourself!

"Whatever you focus on…is your reality!"

I have a friend who is a true entrepreneur. We call him Says Who. Whenever he has some grand idea, we usually say, "You can't do that," and he says, "Says who?" He started a landscaping business in Jacksonville, Florida. If you needed a new deck, patio, or general landscaping, he was the guy to call.

Not too long ago, my friend put in a bid for a multi-million dollar contract. It was the biggest project I had ever seen! All of his friends and family were scared for him—even me! I said to him, "You usually use five or six guys; this will take fifty guys. You deal with budgets in the thousands, and this is in the millions. You can't do this!" And, of course, he said, "Says who?" My friend was focused on his goal and refused to be sidetracked by anything or anyone.

As it turned out, he got the contract. It was for the National Football League and the owner of the Jacksonville Jaguars. He was contracted to remove and replace all the seats in Jacksonville Municipal Stadium. That's over 76,000 seats! He's currently negotiating with the owners of the Orange Bowl in Miami to re-seat their stadium.

My friend taught me a valuable lesson about focus. His own family and friends didn't believe he could do it, including me. But now I realize that extraordinary focus will keep you on track with your goal.

I have a lot of respect for major league baseball players. It's one of the few careers where you will experience much more failure than success. In baseball, if you go up to bat ten times, you might get three hits. That's it: three! Baseball players will fail seventy percent of the time, but somehow they have the persistence to go for that hit the next time they're up.

Hammering Hank Aaron is known as one of the greatest power hitters of all time. But as he got closer to breaking Babe Ruth's homerun record, he actually received death threats. Babe Ruth was an American icon, and there were plenty of people who did not want his record of 714 homeruns to be broken.

On April 8th, 1974, Hank Aaron was able to persevere, and he broke Babe Ruth's record. Before retiring, he went on to hit 755 homeruns. But people often forget: Although Hank had 755 homeruns, he had over 1,350 strikeouts. If Hank Aaron had focused on all his failure, he would have never achieved such success. You can do the exact same thing!

Lesson learned:

Develop extraordinary focus!

Write down three distractions that interfere with achieving your goal.

1.)_____

2.)_____

3.)_____

Write down three ways to focus and overcome those distractions.

1.)_____

2.)_____

3.)_____

"You are what you practice most."

Richard Carlson

Practice Makes Improvement!

We've always been taught that "practice makes perfect." Actually, that is not true! Practice makes *improvement*! You have never seen your best. No matter how hard you've worked, there is always room to improve! The word *practice* is defined as:

"The act of rehearsing a behavior over and over, or engaging in an activity again and again, for the purpose of improving."

Did you catch the words "over and over" or "again and again"? The key to practice is repetition. Never believe you have practiced enough or that you know it all...ever!

"It's the things you learn after you think you know it all that really count."
John Wooden,Legendary UCLA Basketball Coach

Hall of Fame basketball player Michael Jordan would practice free throws with his eyes closed until he could consistently make the shot. He also started a voluntary basketball training camp months before the NBA's mandatory training camp. His voluntary camp became so popular that players from other teams would attend Jordan's training camp to practice.

Question: Do you really think the greatest player in basketball needed that much practice?

Answer: Yes. It's because he practiced so much that he became great!

Think of all the females that you know.
(grandmother, aunt, mother, sister, or friend).

Question: What is the number-one medical concern for females?

Answer: If you said breast cancer, you're wrong. It's heart disease.

Question: If you had heart disease and you could see any doctor in the world, who would you want?

Answer: Dr. Paula A. Johnson.

Dr. Johnson is the first woman to be named chief medical resident at Brigham and Women's Hospital in Boston. In her biography, Dr. Johnson wrote, "I'm constantly evolving like medicine itself. I continue to practice, study, and grow." Dr. Johnson is one of the top cardiologists in the world but she continues to work on her craft.

Question: Do you think one of the best cardiologists in the world needs that much practice?

Answer: Yes. It's because she practices so much that she's one of the best!

Practicing on a regular basis takes commitment and discipline. It also helps you avoid the "yeah, but" disease! This disease gives you excuses not to practice.

Here are the top five excuses!

1.) Yeah, but I can practice later!

2.) Yeah, but my favorite TV show is on!

3.) Yeah, but my friend is calling me!

4.) Yeah, but I don't feel like it!

5.) Yeah, but I don't need to practice anymore!

If you feel like your practice sessions aren't inspiring you, make sure you didn't catch the "yeah, but" disease. The antidote is consistent practice.

Darren Hardy is the publisher of *Success Magazine* and author of the book *The Compound Effect.* According to Mr. Hardy, the key to achievement is consistent effort and practice, which eventually compounds into success. So, if you don't see results right away, don't give up. Keep practicing.

Here are five tips for a successful practice:

1.) Set a regular practice time!
A regular practice time mentally prepares you to practice and keeps you on schedule. You should always know your practice time.

2.) Set a practice length!
If you know your practice lasts one hour, thirty minutes, or even twenty minutes, you can focus and stay consistent.

3.) Have a regular practice place!
The same practice place tells the brain "it's practice time." The same room or area puts you in the right mindset to practice.

4.) Always review, before doing anything new!
This is a great technique for memorization. Before moving on to new material, review everything from the day before.

5.) Reward yourself!
Once you've accomplished a certain task, celebrate a little. Buy some candy, go out with your friends, or go to a movie—anything (within reason) that says "job well done."

Lesson learned:

Consistent practice is the key!

"Genius is one percent inspiration and ninety-nine percent perspiration."

Thomas Edison

Write down three of your school subjects where you need more practice.

1.)_____

2.)_____

3.)_____

Write down three of your extra-curricular activities where you need more practice.

1.)_____

2.)_____

3.)_____

"Success is how high you bounce after you hit bottom!"

General George S. Patton

Dust Yourself Off!

No one likes to talk about this, but all teenagers will experience some failure. To be extraordinary does not mean you avoid failure, it simply means if you experience failure, you need to dust yourself off and move on! I know that sounds easier said than done, but when you are able to keep striving for your goal, even in the midst of failure, that's when you're on the path to being extraordinary. In other words, be persistent!

> *"Only those who dare to fail greatly can achieve greatly."*
> **—Robert F. Kennedy**

Ask yourself these questions:
- Am I persistent?
- Do I finish what I start?
- If I fail at my dream, will I keep trying?

Hopefully, you said "yes" to all those question, but understand this: Life is not going to hand you your dream on a silver platter. Life is going to try to knock you down! So, you've got two choices! You can stay knocked down or you can get back up!

In 1890, Harland Sanders was born in a small town near Henryville, Indiana. As a young boy, he picked up the art of cooking and mastered many dishes by age seven. By 1930, he was regularly cooking for travelers coming through his town looking for a meal.

But Harland had an incredible desire to start his own business. He got the courage to travel by car to different restaurants and cook fried chicken on the spot for restaurant owners—in their restaurant! If the owners liked the chicken, they would pay Harland one nickel per piece of chicken sold. If they didn't like the chicken, it was "get outta my restaurant." He heard over 100 "no's" before he heard his first "yes." Harland was relentless and stayed persistent! He wouldn't give up! That was a good thing because the Governor of Indiana became a fan of Harland's cooking and gave him the honorary title of "Colonel." So we know Harland as Colonel Harland Sanders. Because he was persistent, Colonel Sanders opened his famous Kentucky Fried Chicken (now known as KFC) restaurant all over North America, selling his famous fried chicken.

Persistence is key! It will help you stay on track and avoid the Fed Ex failure! Federal Express! It's the "I need it now" syndrome. Today, we live in a microwave society where everything must arrive in seconds. Your local cable company now offers a power boost Internet speed and smart phones are jumping to 4G speed to keep up with demand. Unfortunately, sometimes we use the "I need it now" syndrome with our goals. Remember, good things take time!

Have you heard of country singer and actor Billy Ray Cyrus? Do you remember his big musical hit "Achy Breaky Heart"? I got a chance to interview him when I was at Fox 5 News. Billy Ray was known as an overnight sensation, but he does not like that title. Why? Because Billy Ray Cyrus was on the road singing in small towns and bars for *ten years* before he got his big break. I'll say that again: ten years! But he continued to work on his goal of being a professional singer even though it was taking a long time.

His story made me realize that sometimes people don't achieve their goals because it doesn't happen fast enough. They'll give up and quit! So, ditch Fed Ex when it comes to your goals. Give yourself the time to develop and grow!

In 1941, after hunting in the Swiss Alps with his dog, scientist George de Mestral noticed sticky burrs all over his clothing and his dog's fur. After examining the tiny objects through a microscope, George was convinced he could use the burrs in a new invention. His first version was introduced in the 1950s but he was told it was impractical. But he stayed persistent and didn't quit! Finally, by 1960, he re-vamped his invention so it could be used by astronauts at NASA. Shortly afterwards, it became a national sensation. The invention was Velcro.

"I don't think there is any other quality so essential to success of any kind as the quality of perseverance. It overcomes almost everything...even nature!."
—John D. Rockefeller

It's really easy to focus on someone's success and fail to see their bumps along the road. There are numerous American icons who have experienced a tremendous amount of failure before seeing success!

Here are some of my favorites:

1.) **Abraham Lincoln lost 7 elections before becoming President.**

2.) **Thomas Edison** failed 1,000 times trying to create the light bulb.

3.) **Ted Turner** (the creator of CNN News) was told twenty-four-hour cable news and sports was a terrible idea.

4.) **"The King" Elvis Presley** was told he had no chance of being a singer and should go back to driving a truck.

5.) **Walt Disney** was told he lacked imagination and had no good ideas.

Lesson learned:

Don't give up...stay persistent!

Write down three of your biggest failures
(school subject, sporting event, musical event, etc.).

1.)_____

2.)_____

3.)_____

**For each failure, write down three new steps you can
take to succeed**
(find a tutor, more practice, better attitude etc.).

1.)_____

2.)_____

3.)_____

"The greatest power that a person possesses is the power to choose."

J. Martin Kohe

It's Your Choice!

"Your choices are a reflection of you." I went to James Madison University in Harrisonburg, Virginia. I remember having a huge biology test on a Friday morning. But out of the blue, my roommate scored four tickets to see the King of Pop Michael Jackson in Washington, DC—the night before my biology test. You must understand: A Michael Jackson concert was a historic event and instant "date material" with any female on campus.

I had a dilemma. I could stay home and study for my test or go to a once-in-a-lifetime epic concert. What should I do?

Answer: I'm going to the concert!

My roommate took his girlfriend Kathy and I took Lara. With a two-hour drive to the Capitol Center, we would need to leave campus by four o'clock Thursday afternoon. We picked up the ladies and headed off to Washington. We had a great time and the concert was awesome! Believe it or not, in a 20,000-seat arena, our seats were in the fourth row. Lara thought I was the king! We got back to campus and our dorm room around 6am Friday morning. I was exhausted! Then I remembered...my test was at 8am!
How do you think I did on my test?

Is there a grade lower than F? That's what I got!
That was the consequence of a poor decision.
The point is that it was my choice to go to the concert.
Your decisions have a lasting effect on your life.

There are times in life when you have to choose between what is right and what is easy. No matter what anyone says, you have *all* the power! You can *choose* to make a good decision or you can *choose* to make a poor decision. It's your choice! And it only takes one poor decision to change your life *forever!*

In 2009, college football star Jeremiah Masoli led the University of Oregon to the Rose Bowl and was considered to be a possible Heisman Trophy candidate. With his popularity growing, he was even featured on the cover of the XBOX 360 EA Sports video game. It seemed like the sky was the limit for Jeremiah, but one poor decision changed everything.

One evening, Jeremiah *made the decision* to break into a fraternity house and steal two laptop computers and a guitar. The Oregon superstar athlete was arrested and charged with a felony for stealing. In addition, police cited him for possession of marijuana and driving with a suspended license.

Have you heard of rap star DMX? In 1999, Earl Simmons, aka DMX, was on top of the hip hop world. His music career was on fire and his new CD went six times platinum. His talents also allowed him to cross onto the big screen, as he was featured in numerous major motion pictures. It seemed like the sky was the limit for DMX, but one night of poor decisions changed everything. One evening, DMX *made the decision* to use drugs and carry a concealed weapon. The rap and movie star was arrested on charges of cocaine possession, criminal possession of a weapon, and driving under the influence of drugs or alcohol.

Jeremiah Masoli and DMX learned hard lessons from their poor decisions. Masoli was kicked off the football team and eventually left the University of Oregon. DMX went to prison.

It is very easy to get wrapped up in the moment and fail to consider the "big picture" of your actions.

Here are three key points to decision making.

You're about to make a poor decision if:

1.) You're making a quick decision!
Very rarely in life will you need to make a quick decision. Take time to *think* before you act. A quick decision = a poor decision.

2.) Your friends or peer group are trying to pressure you!
Think for yourself! If your friends won't respect you and your decision, then they *are not* your friends.

3.) You haven't thought about the consequences!
Think about the consequences of cheating, stealing, lying, drugs, drinking alcohol, or pre-marital sex before you find yourself in that situation. How do you feel about it?

- How would it feel to be in the principal's office for cheating or stealing?
- How would it feel to be in the doctor's office because you contracted a sexually transmitted disease or you're pregnant?
- How would it feel to call your parents from the sheriff's office because you were caught drinking alcohol or doing drugs?

If you've already thought about the consequences of poor decisions, you can't be caught off guard in the moment. Your decisions...good and bad, have a lasting effect on your life.

Lesson learned:

It's your choice...take time to think!

Write down three poor choices you made this year.

1.)_____

2.)_____

3.)_____

Write down three ways you could have avoided those choices.

1.)_____

2.)_____

3.)_____

Additional

Let's keep it real!

Smoking weed, drinking alcohol, carrying a gun or knife, or dealing drugs will end badly for you. Period! You will either end up in prison, in the hospital, or in the grave! Period! It's not cool, it's not hard, it's not real—it's stupid!

Drugs

And yes—alcohol is a drug! Drinking alcohol can lead to some of the worst decisions in your life, such as driving under the influence, misdemeanors, felonies, and violence.

The teen website marijuana-anonymous.org has story after story of teens getting hooked on or dealing marijuana, which in turn destroyed their lives. I specify marijuana because many teens believe this drug doesn't count. After all, it's not as bad as heroin or cocaine, right? Not true

Marijuana use always starts out of curiosity, but eventually you'll end up kicked out of school, out of your home, or you'll end up in prison. As one anonymous sixteen-year-old states on marijuana-anonymous.org, *"It's not worth it!"*

Guns

Carrying a gun takes poor decision-making to another level! Psychologically speaking, carrying a gun gives you a false sense of reality. It's almost as if the gun *thinks for you* and decides your actions!

If someone bumps into you or says something you don't like, what do you do?

A.) If you're *not carrying* a gun, you might make a verbal comment, roll your eyes, or do nothing.

B.) If you're *carrying* a gun, you'll somehow justify in your mind that you have to pull it out. You feel threatened or disrespected so you must retaliate! (That's the gun talking!)

Here's the real problem with guns: The end result is *death*, but you don't think about that. You think about the way the gun makes you feel!

"When you carry a gun, whether you realize it or not...you mean to harm somebody."
—**Bill Cosby**

Carrying a gun makes you feel:

1.) Strong.

2.) Confident.

3.) In Control.

4.) Grown up.

5.) Safe and secure.

And if you use the gun…

6.) Someone is injured.

7.) Someone is *dead!*

Did you notice death is last? That's the problem! When you carry a gun, you're only thinking about numbers one through five, but unfortunately, numbers six and seven are likely to happen!

Many teenagers feel they have to get a gun because the rumor-mill says their enemy at school has a gun. If that is the case, resist getting a gun and *immediately* tell an adult, teacher, or educator!

Understand this: The teenage code of staying quiet and dealing with problems yourself does nothing more than keep *the problem* in charge! Don't stay quiet! And, if you witness a threat to someone else, don't stay quiet. Tell someone! If you see something, say something!

Why? Because there is *no* teenage code—it's a *big lie!*

Think about this:

You are developing into a young adult. And as an adult, if someone physically threatens you or your family, you should call the police. If your house is on fire, you call the fire department. If you witness a medical emergency, you call an ambulance!

Only teenagers have a mythical code where it is better to "man up" and handle possible emergencies *alone*. That is completely backwards! It actually shows maturity to tell someone; it shows you are becoming a young adult. Don't stay quiet—tell someone!

> "The victory of success is half won when one gains the habit of work."
>
> **Sarah Bolton**

Hey, Get a Job!

That's right! Whether it's babysitting, mowing lawns, or working at McDonald's, the time has come for you to work. Other than schoolwork, many teenagers are involved in sports, music, or other extra-curricular activities, making it difficult to have a job, too. If possible, try to find a part-time job on the weekends or over the summer. You need extra money, and employers need dependable and responsible employees. You can find job postings at your local community center, church, newspapers, and, of course, online!

Social media rules our lives! Facebook, Twitter, and Google have created new and instant ways of communication. Instantly, you can research companies, read online message boards, and find new job postings. It's a great way to connect and share information. But, in reality, social media creates good news and double bad news for teenagers!

The good news is you can quickly give your opinion or describe yourself online with instant messages, tweets, posts, photos, and videos.

The bad news is that potential employers will randomly background check your social media pages.

Studies have proven that 60% of potential employers will check your social media profiles. The pictures you post and comments you make are a direct reflection of you. If you're using foul language and posting risqué photos, it doesn't say you're cool! It says you're immature. And potential employers don't have time for immaturity! If you want to be taken seriously by an employer, clean up your Facebook page.

There's more bad news. Because of social media, some teenagers struggle with face-to-face communication in professional settings.

To land a good job, you must learn face-to-face communication skills! Employers want to have a serious discussion with you. You can't send a quick tweet or blog post. You need to look your potential employer in the eye and talk!

Get comfortable talking about yourself. I'm not implying you should brag or be conceited. No one wants to hear how great *you* think *you* are! But be confident about yourself and clearly articulate who you are and what you want!

Fifty-five percent of a potential employer's perception of you is based on how you look. It's an old saying but it's still true: "You never get a second chance to make a first impression."

Quick Tips:

- **Dress for Success!**
When you set out to find a job, dress nice! Don't think you can simply fill out applications and interview on a different day. Often times, the manager will want to interview you that very same day. If you're dressed in shorts and a t-shirt…you just blew it! Dress and act as if the owner of the company wants to speak to you today.

- **Be Prepared!**
You already know that all employment applications are

going to ask for names, home and school addresses, and phone numbers. Make sure you have them! Giving an incomplete application to the store manager sends the wrong message! Also, being prepared means you take time to think *in advance* about the position and the interview.

Here are five common interview questions you should prepare for:

1. **What are your greatest strengths?**
   Example answers:
   Positive attitude, leadership skills, work ethic, team player.

2. **Why should I hire you?**
   Example answers:
   Customer-service skills, hard worker, dependable. Do not compare yourself to other candidates for the position.

3. **What do you know about our organization?**
   Example answers:
   Research the organization before the interview so you'll have an answer handy. Who is the owner? What do they provide or sell?

4. **Why do you want to work for this organization?**
   Example answers:
   Your answer should be based on your research, but be sincere. Your answer could relate to your long-term goals.

5. **What are your long-term goals?**
Your employer understands that you have other aspirations, so be honest.
Example answers:
Go to college; join the military; be a nurse, doctor, web-designer, engineer, or accountant; own a business.

You should already know the answers to these questions, but now you need to be concise and verbalize them in an interview. The teenager that puts some thought behind these questions makes a strong impression with the manager.

- **Create T.O.M.A.**
  — Top-of-Mind Awareness!
"People like to be around people that make them feel good." Think about it! Don't you enjoy hanging around people who are fun and positive? Adults do, too! So be enthusiastic and likeable! T.O.M.A. means you've created such a good impression that you are the logical choice for the job. You're on the top of their minds. You've created T.O.M.A.

Here's a question for you:

According to HR directors and hiring managers,

What is the most challenging part of a job interview?

Answer:
It's when the employer says, "Tell me about yourself."

That's it! This one statement will cause blank stares, um's, well's, uncertainty, and anxiety. You name it. Why? Because most teenagers never truly prepare for this question! And if you're not prepared, it makes you look very uncertain of yourself and unprofessional.
What's the solution?

Create a thirty-second elevator speech!

Imagine you just walked into an elevator full of people. It is so cramped you can barely move your arms. At the second floor, everyone exits the elevator except you and Mark Zuckerberg (the owner of Facebook). At that moment, you realize that you and multi-billionaire Mark Zuckerberg are going to the fiftieth floor—alone! What do you do? What are you going to say? How will you introduce yourself?
Use an elevator speech! It's a quick and concise description of who you are, what you've done, what you're looking for, and how you can help *their* company.

Let's break down the elevator speech.

- **Who you are?**
  Hi, my name is_____, and I'm a junior at Westside High School in Springfield, Virginia.

- **What have you done?**
  I'm a good student and really enjoy _____ and _____.

(e.g., a particular class, sport, musical instrument, etc.) Give a couple of examples of where you excelled.

- **What are you looking for?**
  In a couple of years, I'm hoping to go to college, but for now, I'm looking for a part-time job after school or over the summer.

- **How can you help their company?**
  I'm a very hard worker, a quick learner, and dependable. I'm just looking for an opportunity!

It's your story, so memorize it, know it, and believe it! If you don't believe what you're saying, no one else will, either. Look your potential employer right in the eye and say it with confidence!

The elevator speech is quick and concise. (Thirty seconds.) Don't ramble on! You want to give them time to ask you a question and start a dialogue. You can use the elevator speech when you're interviewing for a job, the military, or college. It's also effective when you're networking with influential people.

Write down your personal "elevator speech."

_____

_____

_____

_____

_____

_____

_____

_____

_____

_____

_____

_____

_____

_____

_____

Congratulations, you got the job. Now it's time to keep the job.

Jennifer was 16 years old and worked part time at an ice cream shop. Like many teenagers, Jennifer only worked at the ice cream shop for extra spending money and had no desire to be in the shop any longer than she had to. One evening, Jennifer was on the closing shift by herself and was told by her store manager to close the store at 9pm. It sounded easy, but there was a problem. Jennifer wanted to go to a party! Not just any party, but the party of the summer! This party was important; this party was going to be epic! She had to be there! So Jennifer had to make a decision. In reality, she could have just closed the shop at 9pm, changed clothes, and arrived at the party a little late.

But instead, Jennifer decided to close the shop early. As she was closing the doors, a customer walked up wanting some ice cream for his family. Jennifer said, "Sorry, we're closing now!" The man looked perplexed and said, "But your sign says you should still be open." Paying him no attention, Jennifer said, "Sorry...have to close early!" She closed the door and went to the party.

Think about it: Jennifer disregarded her manager's instructions, prevented the store from making money by closing early, and lied to the last customer. As it turned out, that last customer was the store manager's brother! **Busted!** *The next day Jennifer found herself in the office trying to explain herself.*

You keep your job by staying professional and *working* when you're at work! You're probably only working part-time hours, anyway, so show up on time wearing pressed, clean work attire, have integrity, and commit to your shift! One last thing—have fun!

As a teen, I worked at Little Caesar's Pizza. My position was called "landing!" When the pizzas came out of the motorized oven and "landed" in my section, I grabbed them! It was my job to take the pizzas out of the pan, put them in the box, and slice! But we had fun! My friends Dave, Chris, and I made up the part-time landing shift. Our nicknames were "the landing boys!" We were famous for yelling call signs like "pizza out!" "on deck!" and "eyes up!" "Eyes up" meant a hot girl just walked in! No one else knew what that one meant...except us. We were crazy!

As you can imagine, "landing" became the most popular spot in the store. Eventually, I left Little Caesar's because I was going to college. But before I left, the store manager told me how much he enjoyed it when the "landing boys" worked. He said we were always positive and made the atmosphere fun and energetic.

I had no idea about the impression we were making just because we had fun! But guess what? When I needed a reference for a job I applied for in college, I called my old pizza manager and he gladly gave me one. So remember: work hard, have integrity, but also have fun. People notice!

Education Pays!

According to the United States Department of Labor, there is a direct correlation between your education and your salary. Adults with at least a bachelor's degree consistently had higher earnings than those with less education. Depending on the industry, the difference in pay will range from 10 to 300%!

The Youth Development and Research Fund states:

The average high school dropout will earn $616,000 over their lifetime.

High school graduates with some community college credits will earn $1,036,000.

College graduates will make $2,000,000.

So by failing to complete high school and college, you potentially lose out on $1,384,000.

Here are the unemployment rates based on education:

- Less than a HS diploma: 11%
- HS diploma: 8%
- Some college, no degree: 5.9%
- Associate degree: 4.5%
- Bachelor's degree: 3.9%
- Master's degree: 2.8%
- Professional degree: 1.9%
  From the Bureau of Labor Statistics Age 25 and over

So, staying in school really *pays off!*

Write down your top five job opportunities.

1.)_____

2.)_____

3.)_____

4.)_____

5.)_____

> "We never appreciate the value of water until the well runs dry."
>
> **Benjamin Franklin**

Have Gratitude!

Have gratitude! The truly extraordinary realize that,
regardless of their present circumstances, whether they
are struggling or not, they are extremely blessed.
It is so easy to forget the blessings of health, family, and
friends. Television and Internet ads slam us with the latest
gadgets, gizmos, and must-haves! If we're not careful,
we'll focus and base our lives on everything we *don't*
have!

I was driving home from work a few years ago after
having a really bad day. It was the middle of the summer
in Las Vegas and about 110 degrees outside. I remember
sitting at a red light on my cell phone, venting to my wife
about how horrible things were. At that moment, I looked
to my left and saw an African-American man with long,
dirty hair and lips severely chapped from the heat. He was
wearing ripped, dirty clothes, one shoe, and was pushing a
grocery cart. And there I was, driving in my air-
conditioned car, going to my house to see my loving wife
and children. I felt at that moment God was giving me a
big dose of perspective.

True Stories!

After swimming in the Tallapoosa River in Georgia, Aimee was diagnosed with a rare, flesh-eating disease. The bacterial infection emits toxins that cut off blood flow to parts of the body. It literally destroys muscle, fat, and skin tissue. She spent weeks on a respirator while undergoing amputations of her left leg, right foot, and both hands. Aimee is eighteen years old.

Mark was a normal, healthy, teenager with dreams of opening his own specialty racecar shop. After visiting the doctor for his high school physical, Mark heard the most shocking news of his life—he had cancer. Mark said, "I've been through hell with all my medical issues. Constant radiation treatment and chemo is not fun. After my latest biopsy, the right side of my body is starting to go numb." Mark is fourteen years old.

Abigail was diagnosed with a brain tumor when she was about two. Today, she can't eat on her own, so she has to use a J-tube (feeding tube.) Also, she can no longer speak, so she uses sign language to communicate. Abigail attends a public high school and needs a nurse and interpreter to follow her around in school. She said, "It's a major social turn off, so most students ignore me. But I have a couple of friends who care enough about me and learned sign language." Abigail is sixteen years old.

Being a healthy teenager is a tremendous blessing! According to cancer.gov, forty-six children or teens are diagnosed with cancer *every single day!* To *be extraordinary* means to be grateful for the blessings you do have.

Studies have proven that if you are relatively healthy, live in a house, have running water or even a working toilet, you're considered to be "better off" than a good percentage of the entire globe! Be grateful!

"You don't have to see the whole staircase...just take the first step."

Dr. Martin Luther King, Jr.

Congratulations!

You just finished your Be Extraordinary roadmap!
But this was just the first step. Now it's time to continue
your journey. Knowledge means nothing unless you take
that knowledge and use it!

Use this book as a resource and review your goals every
few months. Don't be surprised if your goals change!
That's okay! It's absolutely normal to modify or
completely change your goals! But don't change your
goals because they're too difficult or challenging! Your
goals should be challenging!

"In times of adversity, you'll find your character!"

As a teenager, when you hit adversity, you'll have two
choices: You can get bitter or better! That's it! *Choose* to
get better! Playin' the victim is weak! Don't let others
label or define you. Be proud of yourself and allow *you* to
identify who *you* are!

Many teenagers *talk* about changing their life and going
for their dream, but don't take any steps to make it
happen. So today, I challenge you to do what others won't
do, so that tomorrow you'll have what others won't have.

God Bless,

Darryl Ross

Self-Assessment

Take a moment and answer the following four questions.
You'll learn a lot about yourself!

What would I do if I won $1,000,000 today?

_____

_____

_____

_____

_____

_____

_____

_____

Who are the five most important people in my life?

1.)_____

2.)_____

3.)_____

4.)_____

5.)_____

Which one thing would I change about the world and why?

_____

_____

_____

_____

_____

_____

_____

_____

What would I do if I only had six months to live?

_____

_____

_____

_____

_____

_____

_____

_____

Resources

Focus Adolescent Services
Website-based organization that addresses teen issues
ranging from bullying, anger issues, overweight teens,
and runaways.

Healthy Teen Network
Teen pregnancy, prevention, and teen families.
healthyteennetwork.org

Dreams for Kids
A non-profit, charitable organization founded in 1989.The
organization empowers at-risk youth and those with disabilities
through a variety of programs.
dreamsforkids.org

Big Brothers Big Sisters of America (BBBSA)
Five hundred agencies that serve youth with mentors and
role models.
bbbs.org

Jobcorps
The nation's largest residential education and job-training program for at-risk youth.
jobcorps.gov

National Association of Service and Conservation Corps (NASCC)
Membership organization for youth corps programs.
nascc.org

Youthbuild
Over two hundred programs in forty-six states, Washington, DC, and the US Virgin Islands. Sixteen to twenty-four year olds work full-time for six to twenty-four months toward their GEDs or high school diplomas.
youthbuild.org

Americorps
National service program allowing people to earn help paying for education in exchange for a year of service.
americorps.gov

Jobs for America's Graduates (JAG)
Assistance for at-risk youth to graduate high school and
find a job.
jag.org

National 4-H
Non-profit educational organization devoted to creating
programs and opportunities for youth.
4-h.org

National Youth Leadership Council
Creates a more just, sustainable, and peaceful world with
young people, their schools, and their communities
through service learning.
nylc.org

Youth as Resources (YAR)
YAR gives youth an opportunity to take part in
community-service projects.
yar.org
youthasresources.org

Youth Service America
Group of one hundred seventy-one organizations for
community and national service.
ysa.org

Additional websites:

suicide.org

bullying.org

stopbullying.gov

Students Against Driving Drunk
sadd.org

drugfreeworld.org

marijuana-anonymous.org

National Urban League
nul.org

Speaking Engagements

Darryl Ross is available for middle schools, high schools, PTA meetings, and youth events.
For more information, please contact :

Darryl Ross Inc.
www.darrylrosslive.com
Email: darryl.ross@live.com

Meeting planners, college, and youth coordinators:

Energize your group! Straight from the news desk, Darryl Ross is a former Fox 5 News reporter and currently one of the most-requested professional speakers. He's truly an entertainer at heart with a passion for people and service.

Darryl's dynamic and high-energy presentation style makes him a favorite for corporations, colleges, high schools, middle schools, and youth events. With his unique and entertaining style, Darryl shares proven success principles, motivation, leadership, and real-world strategies. Darryl will inspire your group into realizing their own potential.

What they are saying:

"Thanks so much for doing both presentations yesterday. You really do put your soul into it. As I was driving Cheryl back to her office, we discussed your presentation and agreed that it was the most powerful one that we have provided for our clients to date. We would love to have you back for a follow-up/additional topic presentation in mid-March or April. Let me know your availability and I will schedule you."

Derick Malis
Project Manager
Phoenix Houses of the Mid-Atlantic

"If you're looking to motivate, inspire, and empower your audience, then you need to hire my friend, Darryl Ross. He has a great heart and truly cares about making a positive difference in the lives of others!"

James Malinchak
Co-Author, *Chicken Soup for the College Soul*

"Darryl's energy and excitement kept the staff from our agency highly engaged and enthusiastic about learning. His commitment to making all of us see the 'big picture' is refreshing. We're excited and can't wait to host him again for this coming spring and summer."

Kristina Savoy,
Program Manager
Department of Consumer & Regulatory Affairs, DC

"Darryl's ability to engage and excite employees about setting individual goals to achieve personal outcomes is unparalleled. Darryl truly has a unique gift of being able to quickly connect with the audience to deliver important information."

Marshall Henson
Vice President
Workforce Development
Linden Resources

"Darryl Ross was dynamic! Our students hung on his every word and made our career day a complete success."

Stephanie Keebler, Principal

Titusville Senior High School

"We haven't seen our students stop talking and pay attention as much as they did with Darryl. We really appreciate his insightful words. He was very inspiring for the students."

Young Scholar's Academy

Fort Mohave, AZ.

"Be Extraordinary"
Book & CD Pack

"Jumpstart Your Success"

Contributing author Darryl Ross, along with top speakers, shares insights for creating more success, wealth, and happiness. *Jumpstart Your Success* also features the legendary Brian Tracy and *Chicken Soup for the Soul's* James Malinchak.

"Be Extraordinary" (Audio)

In this audio CD, Darryl Ross shares his proven ten-step roadmap to success. You'll be energized and motivated to develop your own potential. Follow these fundamentals, tips, and strategies so you can "Be Extraordinary."

To order, please visit: www.darrylrosslive.com

Notes

Notes

Notes

Notes